I0815587

Star Wars

by Julie Murray

Abdo Kids Jumbo is an Imprint of Abdo Kids
abdobooks.com

abdobooks.com

Published by Abdo Kids, a division of ABDO, P.O. Box 398166, Minneapolis, Minnesota 55439.

Printed in the United States of America, North Mankato, Minnesota.

102025

012026

Photo Credits: AdobeStock, Alamy, Everette Collection, Getty Images, Shutterstock, ©ChrisM70 p.7/CC BY-NC-ND 2.0, ©Doug Kline p.15/CC BY-NC 2.0, ©The Retro Spirit p.15/CC BY-NC-ND 4.0, ©TooMuchDew p.15/CC BY-NC-ND 2.0

Production Contributors: Teddy Borth, Jennie Forsberg, Grace Hansen
Design Contributors: Candice Keimig, Pakou Moua

Library of Congress Control Number: 2025936511

Publisher's Cataloging-in-Publication Data

Names: Murray, Julie, author.

Title: Star Wars / by Julie Murray

Description: Minneapolis, Minnesota : Abdo Kids, 2026 | Series: Toy mania! | Includes online resources and index.

Identifiers: ISBN 9798384907602 (lib. bdg.) | ISBN 9798384908302 (ebook) | ISBN 9798384908654 (read-to-me ebook)

Subjects: LCSH: Classic Star wars--Juvenile literature. | Star Wars action figures--Juvenile literature. | Star Wars films--Collectibles--Juvenile literature. | Space toys--Juvenile literature. | Hasbro Entertainment (Firm)--Juvenile literature. | Toys--Juvenile literature. | Toys--History--Juvenile literature.

Classification: DDC 688.72--dc23

Table of Contents

Star Wars

The first Star Wars movie, now called *Star Wars: Episode IV – A New Hope*, hit screens in 1977. It was a huge success. What followed changed the toy world forever!

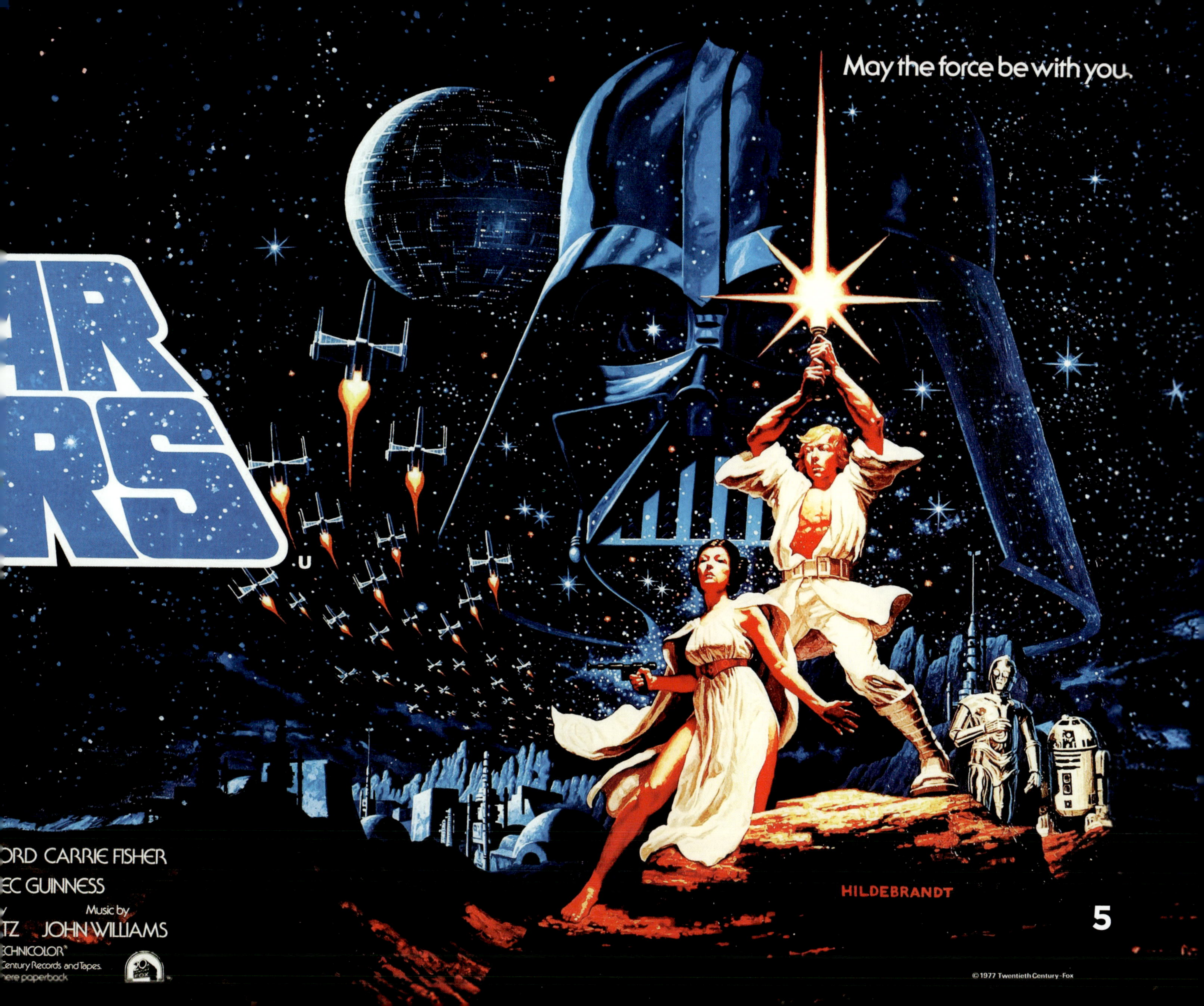

May the force be with you.

AR
RS

U

ORD CARRIE FISHER

EC GUINNESS

Music by

TZ JOHN WILLIAMS

CHNICOLOR®

Century Records and Tapes.

here paperback

HILDEBRANDT

The First Wave

Writer and **director** George Lucas created Star Wars. He wanted toys to go along with his film. He joined forces with Kenner Products. The first wave of Star Wars action figures was released in 1978.

George Lucas

Excited fans bought Early Bird **Certificates**. These were sold during the 1977 holiday season. Fans could trade their certificates for the action figures once they hit store shelves.

STAR WARS™

AGES 4+

85749

EARLY BIRD CERTIFICATE PACKAGE

...e only - offer expires December 31, 2005.

INCLUDES:

- ★ EARLY BIRD CERTIFICATE -- good for updated versions of the first authentic set of four *STAR WARS* Action Figures
- ★ Colorful Display Stand with *STAR WARS* Picture
- ★ *STAR WARS* Club Membership Card
- ★ *STAR WARS* Stickers
- ★ Hyperspace Trial Membership Certificate
- ★ Pre-addressed Envelope

WHAT YOU DO:

MAIL IN. . .
the enclosed Early Bird Figure Redemption Certificate to be postmarked by November 30, 2005.

RECEIVE. . .
between May 1, 2005 and December 31, 2005, poseable Action Figures of Luke Skywalker™, Princess Leia™, Chewbacca™, and Artoo-Detoo™ while supplies last (see back of package for full details).

STAR WARS

EARLY BIRD

CERTIFICATE PACKAGE

·For a limited time only·
offer expires December 31, 2005

1 of 50,000

Twelve figures came out in the first wave. They were 3.75 inches (9.5 cm) tall and had movable parts. They were very popular!

Ages 4 and up.
STAR WARS
Jawa
Palitoy

As more Star Wars movies were released, more toys hit the shelves. Bigger toys were also released, such as vehicles like the X-Wing Fighter!

AT-AT Walker

AT-ST
Walker
X-Wing
Fighter

Ruling the Toy Galaxy

Hasbro began to sell Star Wars toys in 1991. New movies sparked more interest in the toys. Video games, board games, and even LEGO sets helped grow the Star Wars world.

LEGO
STAR WARS
THE FORCE AWAKENS
LICENSED BY
Nintendo
SUPER
STAR WARS
JVC
STAR WARS
Bally
LEGO
75258

The Black Series toy line **debuted** in 2013. It included action figures, vehicles, lightsabers, and other **collectible** items. Fans loved how well the toys were made and how real they looked!

STAR WARS

Disney bought Star Wars in 2012. Disney's Star Wars movies, video games, and TV shows have paved the way for fresh stories, characters, and toys.

The force of Star Wars can still be felt today. From small action figures to giant playsets, there are always new Star Wars toys coming to a galaxy near you!

STAR WARS
STAR WARS
STAR WARS
STAR WARS
MINECRAFT
clearance

More Facts

- More than 300 million Star Wars toys were sold between 1977 and 1985!
- The **rarest** Star Wars toy is the Rocket-Firing Boba Fett made by Kenner Products. Only about 100 were made. In 2024, one of the toys sold for more than 1 million dollars!
- Star Wars action figures were **inducted** into the National Toy Hall of Fame in 2012.

Glossary

certificate – a piece of paper showing ownership.

collectible – an object that is important enough to be collected, such as a special toy.

debuted – presented for the first time.

director – a person who guides the making of a movie, play, or other show.

inducted – brought in as a member.

rarest – the most uncommon.

Index

Visit **abdokids.com** to access crafts, games, videos, and more!

Use Abdo Kids code

TSK7602

or scan this QR code!